little wife: the story of gold

An autobiography in poems

Nuova Wright

2023 The Calliope Group

ISBN: 979-8-9866015-2-6 (Trade Paperback)
ISBN: 979-8-9866015-1-9 (eBook)

Library of Congress Control Number: 2023930408

Covery Art: David James, The Field of Yellow Flowers

Praise for little wife

"*little wife* travels the liminal space between forgetting and memory, traversing the tough geographies and sites of memory mapped by thinkers such as Carol Boyce Davies, Dionne Brand, and Toni Morrison. Remembering, as imagined in *little wife*, 'doesn't end. Just exhausts' even as it continues to map the humanity of blackness."

Rachel Burgess—author of "Feminine Stubble," "Academic Rock Star," and "On Having a J-O-B"

"Nuova Wright's stunning reflection on sexual trauma is a tornado chase through gauzy and overlapping memories in which anything can happen, and anything does. Here is an Oklahoma of oil and wind and cigarettes, . . . of the natural disaster of generational violence stirred by the secrets mere living struggles to allow . . . If memory, we learn, decides importance, 'the only necessity is/ remembering.'"

J. Reuben Appleman—author of *The Kill Jar*

A Note on the Text

Portions of this work originally appeared in the serial poem *auto: commands: biography*. The poem became part of the unpublished manuscript, *inverted girl* (2005).

auto: commands: biography was nominated for the 2004 Grolier Poetry Prize.

Dedication

For my family: the Johnsons, the Wrights, and everyone in between. Thank you for being stubborn and steady as Earth.

For my village. Thank you for holding me as I fell apart to create this.

For Anissia West, without whom this book would not have made it into the world. Thank you for believing in me.

For my child. Thank you for speaking to me since before you were born.

For my Mama. Thank you for helping me write this.

"If you tell the truth, you don't have to remember anything."
Mark Twain

voices

Narrator/self: I talk to myself often.

ancestral chorus: We keep the real score.

Mama: Mhm, cheers.

unconscious futureself: I wish I'd trust at least one of us.

This is a queer love story.

It is not a loud-and-proud, rainbow-colored love story.

This story starts in a middle class neighborhood
on the Black side of a city
that once burned
the Black side
to ashes.

This story starts with a little girl in that neighborhood.

A little girl with asthma and a love for yellow.

Immediately was a baby.
Not a current situation like
        #lunchtimeselfie or resetting your password
but like a mother has a baby
and simultaneously the mother is mine.

A woman has mother and job and husband
and (immediately) baby in sanitized room.
What did her face look like I assume it was big.

> *out of her mouth speaking language*
> *of situations happen in her head*
> *out of head the pictures of things*
> *happening their way out of a mouth*
> *a page*

Fast forward.

A woman talking loudly.
A woman is laughing loudly
and is tall and is your mother for
all you know.

> *this has something to do with power*
> *and nothing to do with being in a diner*

(mark this spot)

Woman waving her head loudly
is all you need to know of ownership

She kisses your forehead
Sleeping on small bed
Magic woman,
the big one,
there all the time,
so you are hers and she is yours

Sometimes a man is smiling into the face of a little girl and
she
doesn't know who he is.

He says Daddy   and immediately   expects something.

"daddy: do you know what that word means?"

Little girl looking at him a certain way
as reaction.
Possession sits down at language
in this too-white glow-bright diner.
An exchange.

She is a little girl not knowing what to say the way
no little girl should be thinking about what is right
to say:

A little girl vomited
A little girl hit her teacher

Yes, but—

this one, she got sand in her hair
needed to explain.

>A little girl is told to tell her mother she now has breasts.
>Responsibility: a series of gerunds activate systems of should.
>A little girl tells her mother that she now has breasts.

Narrator,
You are a person
like when people look at you, but
say something.
Look at people when they are not looking read another book
smart girl
Look, the funny pictures

poems about purple clouds make teachers tell
little girls they are smart = language of what can be done

>*Great great grandmother nods:*
>*down the line, a little girl reading and writing*
>*is everything*
>*is language of rebelling against what they took*

Pause this.

it is hard to know
what of this story
to tell

even though i am louder
i am not safer
even being less afraid

does not make me safer
does it

The situation is a mother tells a little girl
"your father is dead."
Little girl looking a certain way
as reaction. Says "ok"

Your mother is crying you offer her coffee because she is
yours
in the diner you feed her pancakes they are delicious.
you write her poems and wear a little yellow sleeper she
likes to see you in it.
She is drunk that night, and smiling.

Rewind.

She is dead.
          That a little girl lives with her grandmother
          could mean the woman who owned her as mother is gone
          coffee is gone. Sip another sip anyway.

Narrator: you were tired young.
You hated your fucking grandmother.

Is it language as filter?
what you choose to write of remembering
and the stuff to which you say nevermind?

Is this the language of memory?

Skip. 10 seconds.
Narrator, you become what you fear most.
A mother.
Call this "embodied remembering."

A boy to look at you like you looked at her
The big one
Wide and loud and the expanse of the sky above a tiny head

A secret world, exhausted, just the two of you, always together
you are always there so you are his and he is yours
But pause.

He is not what you'd hoped.
He is everything you'd hoped
for nine years but then
     suck your tongue to swallow what he's lost
becomes a hurt wider than you can hold

a little boy saying everything. not like you. a fighter.
not shy, just hidden. a wailing ache. a refusal: tries to die.

**strong fingers on knife handle you must become
stronger to snatch away what is it with mothers and
snatching to keep their children today I remember**

irony.)

Back arrow key.
To Lizzo performing at your elementary school. The year is 1987.
School gym stage rows of silently awed children mildly horrified
   adults.

>   "I was born like this, don't even gotta try…"
>   Fat woman preens familiar-loud
>   deconstructs wedding dress
>   by having one
>   wearing impossible fabric
>   as flag of reclamation
>   plays flute subverts body code

Body meaning. Little girl sits criss-cross applesauce
      it was indian style back then you could say indian style
roly-poly thighs constrict stares at woman
singing from unknown place

>   the place her mother laughed from
>   wore a silky dress from

*what does that mean I'm just a child how should I know what
the place is?*

Today, sentences placing stickpins in what would be different if you
born later or seen sooner

hold it there, child, your grandmother says.
she dead now not dead then

>   "I'm the pudding in the proof, gotta blame it on my juice"

would maybe never say this lived straddled between eat another
   piece and suck your tummy in

Memory: make anything.

goodbye, little wife

I am the 1st and 2nd and 3rd:
Forks clanking and coffee.

Listen:
Once a girl went to prom in a dark blue dress she said she made it
herself but didn't. It was raining. There were chocolates and little
foods.

> She was in love with him the way a girl
> puts on a pretty blue dress for dancing and is in love
> but he does something. *will you write*
> *what it is?* He makes her cry.
> This is not the fucking memory.

What does it smell like who knows what it smells like?
It smells like a thousand perfumes
and new satin (cheap kind)
tired feet
and sweat.

It was actually beautiful. In that cheating way that twinkle
lights make anything beautiful. But also more than that. A
creamy marble staircase and the glowing constellation of
night skyline through every window. The dim and sparkle
made it special. I wanted to feel at home in that specialness.
I wanted to feel like a string of lights wrapping a mahogany
banister: gold.

You have proven nothing about the memory.
Narrator, tonight you will throw away your prom dress.
Music playing run up and down the stairs to dance.

This is a lie.

The first thing every baby must do
Upon birth
Is
Cry.

The cry provides proof of the ability to breathe.

Evidence is important in states like Oklahoma.

The doctor may bear witness to babies' first breaths, but are
never around the first time fathers and mothers and uncles and
cousins and family friends and blurred nighttime shapes wrench it
away—

I was diagnosed with asthma at age two.

little wife began her training when I was one. W/we were One.

W/we share lungs. It gets complicated.

I am not the 1st and 2nd and 3rd like
I stood at a lectern and announced:
Someone's virginity has been lost in church.

Whole congregation genuflect in the creaky polished pews
looking for it.
This is humor.

A boy sneaks out of morning service with a girl's virtue this is
cheap but still funny you are about fourteen.

Fast forward: to your mother dead.

She would think this *cheap but funny.*

His sweater was beige and nice-looking your pantyhose itchy.
This boy does not leave church with your virginity, but the idea of
it you are kissing in the men's lounge, kissing in the parish library.
Hand on your itchy hose hold breath as someone passes.
**The strange wood grain paneled walls, the smell of older
people and too-oily food. Somehow even the fluorescents
aredingy, proof that worship is not an aesthetic and neither
is secrecy.**

Your father ("daddy: do you know what that means?") in another
room shakes head knows why boys in nice sweaters hold hands

> can't tell you
> didn't stay long enough to say
> watch out for boys who treat you the way I would've
> treated your mother   *any girl really*

every father's hypothetical shotgun
as proof of who they know
they are

Pause. Rewind to congregation praying loudly
for your maidenhead, a HALLELUJAH chime played backward.
You serve them coffee you serve them little foods in the diner

sometimes I go rigid.
tense my knees.
brace to steady myself
or fall as best I can
to curl small
and silent.

that is little wife in me.

my silent sister. *No. No.*

my nettie.

hopping to at the scent
of danger.
making right /and quick!/
to soften my blows.

protecting me.

~~Holding you down.~~

This is the situation.
A little girl gives away all her toys at school does not lose her
virginity in church.
Narrator, you sit just so—this is what is writing the guilt.
Think: both parents gone and she alone to figure.
Think: Angela Davis t-shirt and $20,000 insurance for college.

> *narrativity, end here other things happen*
> *but end here this signifies memory's continuity*
> *press stop fast forward go rewind*
> *things disintegrate stop continue*

She was the most beautiful woman I had ever seen.
Vivid Oshun saffron, cherry red curls, powder blue sweater. She laughed like grey finch keening song.

She was wearing a red *(blood fire root chakra screaming dissociating blood always blood)* nightshirt when she died.

In the emergency room, a white doctor fidgeted as he told us sorry.

We did everything we could, he said.

"ok"

Always, remember?

I must.

I saw her rolling in the street she was eight years old teaching herself to rollerskate metal-wheeled derby things wrong for concrete but she wanted to learn I watched her become woman older than me larger my eyes sunk deep into her face but so sad I sucked my tongue trying to swallow what she'd lost she rolled hip over hip and the bodies of ghosts beneath the pavement rose gasping barbers and doctors fathers and shoeshines conked ladies in fine dresses bloody children floated up to touch my child as through a membrane of water belly to belly raspy-breathed gathering against her skin until she stood up covered in them I nearly snatched her that day a wide-eyed girl all calf legs and laughter almost dragged her back inside to save her from lapping mouths clinging torsos of ancestors and what could I have said to her then wound up in terror's fist as I locked the door behind us? could I have honestly told her to her wet-weary face not to play outside again because it's too dangerous not to learn to skate or bike because the past is hungry

Narrator, you walk into a light-
filled signifier. The narrator walks in,
iced tea, sits in her regular spot.

Remember: Rule of remembering:
Begin somewhere.

I remember the red nightshirt she wore when she died o I
watched her die lovely and hard single mother armed with
cigarettes and a final breath a toast to the breath (today I
thought about

Twenty-one and afraid of her face the day
a girl cuts bare of chemicals
Her mouth a cone
Signifier: afro

Narrator, I shaved my head and now memory is all
curly Qs of meaning on my skull.
What makes a rememberer
share exact things?
Narrator thinking of pizza, pause
and eat.

We'll start again.

Anyway, back to me. Age ten, let's say. Why not?

Age ten.

My mother has died. ~~Given up. I'm not angry, Mama. But you did give up.~~

So much happens before,

but this.

This is the brittle twist of my life. The crack.

This is the bruise I cannot stop feeling.

She was my only anchoring point. All that stopped me from drowning ~~in fat and weird and ugly and cruel joke laughter and strange blurring jeering faces~~ was

her.

And now she's gone.

Inside me, I said, "ok."

I must always be ok. (You were trained, little wife.)

I don't want to explain why.

Not yet.

Bonny girl, bonny girl
You so shy!
Touch your cousin's
face, bring the light back up to it –
don't you want one
just like him?

(Narrator: she wants one just like him.)

and there was a twisting storm all texas electric and it was him that I came for how I know natural disasters tell what people won't today I figured out

      —want him to love her that way!
Bonny girl daddyless,
touch of a face all you got to desire
      and that's a sin

Exegesis of ethics:
Girl, you are lonely
Girl, it look like cocoa to touch

Brawl of black skin,
Beneath is a protector. *(this is ownership.)*

Bonny, bonny thing sad girl
touch and vomit him
back of sin's head is smooth,
snake wheeze out of the memory:

If you are cleaned by admitting it,
bathe in the accident.
Call this "found memory."

I was six years old when I first saw you. That's ripe old in pretty little high yella thang years.

It is foreign. To look now at the camera footage

photographs, you mean?

Yes. Of what I was then.
Sleek and gold and so bright.
Bright as water.

The man my Mama loved wanted me to be neat about my room.

It wasn't seeing, little wife. I didn't see you.

I felt you.

I felt you wake up.

Art of Confession:
Say it. Run!

you were thirteen years old and wanted to love him it was a sin this
is what you learned of love at thirteen playing pregnant vehicle of
your solitude body your god body what girl learns of offering mourn
mingled thing mourn his love you not as wrong as you thought (today
you came to terms with

Denied words creak like old
limbs—stretch away like paper.
Outside the page, memory thick dreck.
It touches you because you thought it.
Stop touching it.

Textual exegesis:
we are a bad girl.

Rewind.
She went to college.
Narrator, you went to bed.
Out the tent of night a girl walking
has overslept her own salacious fun.

Tell people: "I don't know how I made it"

*I remember saying I don't know how I made it but I don't
remember thinking I don't know how I will make it I wonder
if I am lying I wonder if she wondered if she would make it
(today I thought about*

parallels.

Curled in the sheets as an act of prayer
or mimic of a mother
in a red nightshirt:
Does the memory create this, or God?

Narrator: she had her own way of leaving,
Do we call this "memory symmetry"?

/from thence He shall come to judge
the quick and the dead/

She dies!
Narrator, O how you die!

There is a dusty choking spirit that sits on the back of us.

Us. *The purest.* **The Child Spirits.**

A contortionist memnoch.

An author wrote about it once. Many have tried to describe its sticky gouged open eyes and fray-steel teeth settling into our fleshes.

Easy, in this language, to dismiss the symbolic because connotation tries to pretend the symbolic is the opposite of real.

Imaginary.

Shhh. Listen, Children.

Your body cannot lie to you.

Your imagination is Real.

On the days she was awake, the women taught her love.
Narrator, we have reconfigured your
college year settings to sound like
A Handmaid's Tale.
Guy in coffee shop laughs.
He takes our glass.

Breakfast at midnight, breakfast at three:
little girl not knowing what to say the way a woman self drinks
a thousand lemon cokes
and loves.

Coffee shop iced tea: symbol of love.

If memory decides what is important,
the only necessity is
remembering.

Did I tell y'all I have a son?

I don't. But it is still true.

Life cracked him inside, quick as pin bones.

It happened early, just like with me.

That is how I know he is mine.

I can't give him much else but the promise

that he is always mine.

Always a dandelion to me. (*A Russian sunflower. A brilliant owl. A compassionate granny. A Rebel Child Spirit. An avenger. A justice reaper.*

A gentle, delicate child. Tall and small and so perfectly sacred. To be adorned with love. To receive love as justice.)

Someday I hope he sees goldenrod glimmering in his reflection.

(I believe you are waking up, my little one. Mama is fixing it, so you can wander

safely

into healing)

HA HA HA HA HA HA HA HA HA HA HA HA HA HA HA HA
WE ARE ALL THE SAME

SIX SHADES OF FORTUNE'S FOOL

watch.

pan in. a woman crying. do not watch this for five minutes.

If you do, she will die of arbitrary landscape.
She's dead in the white of the day.
(no one in the coffee shop laughs.)
Juicy. Red. Thing. Of a woman crying
Pan out till she is tiny.
Tiny woman tears
Tiny breath

What happens *when the memory could be anyone's?*

If it is spiritual this crying she is salved

Narrator: Rule of Remembering:
it doesn't end. just exhausts.

Playing chase is a child's most natural
introduction to the unyielding chaos
of the universe.
Its bright pulses of love
and humid hissing meanness
fly in drunken tandem,
play switch-a-roo,
don each other's clothes
to send us Children
bursting into jade fields of playground
and gray oceans of concrete sidewalk
wild with pursuit
and ecstasy, both
rebelliously blind.

Unlike Tag's rules and order,
Chase is a lawless place.
Liminal.

Buzzing with potential of touch and tackle and squeeze and
pinch.

Anything can happen there.
Anything does.

Did you know the demise of my family followed the demise of the Arkansas River?

Tulsa's mud-choked Mississippi feeder caught fire in 2005.

My family's hallowed bomb shelter: 2010.

The river fire started when local refinery oil leaked thick sheen across the sluggish un-dammed water surface.

My grandmother's house caught flame as I sat on the floor. Outside, my uncle flicked his cigarette butt and it slow-swallowed the bones in dry September wind.

Oil and wind and cigarettes.

Oklahoma symbols.

My name is ~~miamiapumpkineater~~. I was seven years old when it occurred to me that girls were like flowers. I had seen the grass of the neighborhood park buried beneath a snowfall of dandelions.

Probably more than once. Memory consolidates and bends.

Goldenwild. The little yellow flowers littering the park. I imagine I may have gone to sleep that night thinking of the color. Maybe I tried to explain it to Mama. Maybe I didn't. I was shy.

One day at school, I watched a tawny light-skinned Black girl with "good hair" skip out into the playground sunlight.

Goldenwild again.

She was a dandelion. A field of them. Of course I stared.

Beauty calls to our stares, and that is a neutral truth. One children are allowed to accept. For a little while.

Not long after, I learned to stop staring. I ~~don't~~ know why.

Fast-forward to you
been proving this point for too long.

Her mother and her first love walk into hyperbole.
Mama, this is not the iced tea you like.

What you call that poem?
                    nothing to offer you.
What you tell that lover?

                    dying of shit to say to you.

Put on your thin-girl body,
bonny girl with tits like textual analysis,
make all those boys love you.

*don't think I ever knew to call him daddy man with a bucket
of strawberries we ate and were sick together is not con-
firmed as true but I own it today I wondered*

If memory were truth or possession,
why is it called memory
instead of?

Far too early, I came to know I wasn't a dandelion.
How does a child feel ugliness in their body?
Even here, I thought I knew.

No child should ever feel ugliness in their body.
That is the obvious answer, but let's be realistic.

*Too bright, baby. They didn't understand so they hurt you. I'm so
sorry, little one.*

I could never be dandelion.

too shy and too book smart and too weak and too scared and too
fat

Who could love something like that?

**Too much he loved you they loved you too much it soured
and soiled itself I couldn't explain before—**

Someone should tell mothers they can hurt their babies
even as they try with all their pained and ginger
delicacy not to do so.

Mama. Why didn't you ever tell me?

We are all fools, aren't we? Mothers are far too powerful

to be so damn vulnerable.

cheers.

Oh.

You're right.

You did tell me. Just after you died. ~~I know now, Mama. You were no coward. Just old. Grown old so young.~~

Violence makes 30 feel ancient.

Ask the Rebel Children *(hendrix basquiat tupac holiday smith*

artists in every genre
search for ways
to communicate
their suffering.

It is hard to know what to tell of this story and what not to tell. Even spirits sometimes will shush you.

This is, after all, a queer love story.

This story starts with a little Black girl in the center of America.

The buckle of a very well-known belt. One that has whooped on many.

So of course there is a lot of shushing **like asthma. Like a lung squeezed 'til a vein in the hand pops. 'Til the throat will not swallow**

you didn't listen

Quiet now.

We'll start again, then.

i ate honeysuckle and then
i rubbed my eye. eye swole up.
k—, you were there.

Against the technicolor green of Mama Pat's backyard, we were sparkling ochre things. All limbs and blur of movement. I used to think that mulberry bush held the clothesline upright. Used to think the cracked concrete patio and that cast iron grill were the sum of the world-

orange light behind an eye that can't open.
this light is
what writing memory is.

"We are not obligated to be anything they want us to be. Even when 'they' is us." - Toni Morrison   *<seriously??* **Mama, I'm kidding**

what happened viscous slipping through fissures
of the parts brain forgets
and the parts it rearranges
a collage. an apartment living room.
Mama, you can't smoke in restaurants anymore.
waitress always makes more coffee forks clanking.

~~I didn't want my story to have a~~

~~Man.~~

Psh. Girl, you know better.

Marking him out will do no good.

I eventually grew weary from the hospital stark fluorescent cruelty of Black men.

Of brown arms strong enough to squeeze me 'til freedom and incarceration came away fuzzy, watery, same:

a cicada hum of surreality.

I grew tired of being old. I went looking.

but there is
a man. there was.

There always is.
Mothers. Please.

he grabbed my hand
and pulled me through
a topiary maze of sunflowers
and glass
through cold creek water
spinning backward
falling through the past
we are groomed to repeat
yanking me dizzy
past myownself
made me run
choking to chase
me down

Hello, little wife.
Hey, little enemy.
Will we never get along,
You and I?

There were so many girls. Innumerable flowers scattered across schoolyards and corner stores and park swings. Swaying.

I envied them and longed for them and longed to be them, just as I did with my mother. **And Mama, how I was you. How you were me. How we twined like twizzlers around one another**

two fine redbone riding hoods in hoods run by Nezuko wolves

I still may not fully know how to love without ~~idolizing~~ pushing away.

~~I didn't know to call it love for so long.~~

They're all so sorry. You're all so sorry. I hear you. I know.

Yes, I forgive you all.

Yes, even you.

Now go.

Boys were beautiful too. But cruel.

Stern glances. Dark stubbled jaws. That liquor sour and jaudice eye. Questions drunk on demanding.

They were the ones I was supposed to love.
So I did.

Only they could save me from how Wrong I was. How Not
Dadelion. *(They could never save you, babygirl. little wife. Brown
arms were the only devil you knew*

and the world was heaven-less)

I would find a way to circumnavigate their hollow glares
and make one love me.

Their cruelty a love I was safe to have.

Abuse is called a lot of strange nicknames.

(Like Daddy.
Like brother.
Like Pastor.
Like Officer.
Like sir.
Like son.
Like lover-

Narrator, you crumble magnificently
collapse fantastic crack open like panic grew legs you terrified no
mama to tell you what to do you don't know how to

make him want to stay.

Neat rows of dark lines on brown thigh sunken eyes
Narrator, O how he try to die

serves you right God gave you a baby born bright to grow
a closed room of screaming in his belly
serves you just right he is how you learn

nobody teaches little black kids how to (want to) stay alive

Children of Oshun. Of Isis. Of Ma'at.
Brilliant Children.
Golden Ones.

They (we) are the ones forced to suffer most.

A flaw in the system, really. Human fragility is natural. Spirits forget.

**Well, they shine too brightly, these Ones. Bite like baby
copperheads**

*a burst of pure opalescent beauty
unbearable
seems to shatter adult minds
in too many ways
too many*

You. We. I. Experienced all of them.

It doesn't take long to get old.

Time is not what we think it is.

thank you, little wife.
you can rest now.
our Mama got us.
Go. Now.

we're safe, sister wife.
little beast of duty
and devotion.

let go.
a field of wildflowers
and thrumming bees
and curious insects
waits for you.

Go *in* peace. Go *in* flames. GO.

Do *not* come back.

Play. 1.25X speed.
The memory will never say exactly what you meant.

Narrator: today is your birthday.

> *when she contracts, spread open –*
> *birth as eclipse into your first*
> *chilly fluorescent sunlight*
> *maybe then the vocabulary will become*

enough.)

Epilogue: your language will not translate into what she
          meant by love
will never be the exact thing we meant to serve
our compasses of light
our corporeal

the communion of saints

the forgiveness of sins

the resurrection of the body

and the life everlasting

The narrator would like to apologize
for her mother.
She kissed you,
wound up the oxygen behind
your spinal column

> *this was not an asthma attack
> and will not bring her
> back to you*

Strung pretty syllables around
~~your neck~~   *no*

a grave

and she still doesn't
come for you

rather watches from the kitchen
yearning for those rituals of
cooking   sex   cigarette
the red badge
of satisfaction

*the loves of our dead
are faceless dollars*

Anyway, sorry we fainted

Special Thanks

To Quraysh Ali Lansana for your invaluable eyes and energy in helping me bring this book to life. To Shawn Crawford and The Calliope Group for giving it a home. Thank you, thank you, thank you.

Bio

Nuova Wright is a Tulsa, Oklahoma native who earned their MFA in Poetry from Boise State University. Their poems have appeared in *Santa Clara Review*, *Spill Words*, *Elephants Never*, *Please See Me*, *Q/A Poetry*, *The Girl God*, *Word Riot*, *This Land*, as well as on countless restaurant napkins. Wright is a two-time Pushcart Prize nominee and was a 2004 Grolier Prize finalist as well as the author of three poetry chapbooks. Wright has taught at Houston Community College, Tulsa Community College, University of Tulsa, and Street School Tulsa. They are the proud mother of one phenomenal child.